Ma0079500

Other books in the series:
The Crazy World of Birdwatching (Peter Rigby)
The Crazy World of Gardening (Bill Stott)
The Crazy World of Golf (Mike Scott)
The Crazy World of Jogging (David Pye)
The Crazy World of Love (Roland Fiddy)
The Crazy World of Marriage (Bill Stott)
The Crazy World of Photography (Bill Stott)
The Crazy World of Rugby (Bill Stott)
The Crazy World of Sailing (Peter Rigby)
The Crazy World of Sex (David Pye)
The Crazy World of Skiing (Craig Peterson & Jerry Emerson)
The Crazy World of Tennis (Peter Rigby)

Published in Great Britain in 1988 by Exley Publications Ltd,
16 Chalk Hill, Watford, Herts WD1 4BN, United Kingdom.

Reprinted 1990

ISBN 1-85015-111-3

Printed and bound in Hungary.

the CRAZY world of MUSIC

Cartoons by
Bill Stott

⧉ EXLEY

"O.K. Grandpa, I've finished. You can take out the earplugs now."

"Me? I'm with your brother-in-law. That's the worst xylophone I ever heard."

"Bass guitar? I hadn't realized Schumann wrote anything for bass guitar ..."

"Now we'd like to sing ... 'Hey, there goes our agent with the cash!'"

"Wagner's not your thing, then?"

"Isn't that your piano teacher?"

"*Turn it down or I'll tell your father what you said about Kiri Te Kanawa.*"

"Your speakers are all burned out and you can't afford to get them fixed?
Oh my – what a shame!"

"If music be the food of love, I've got indigestion..."

"O.K. Hand it over."

"He's playing the piano. The piano's winning ten-nil."

"O.K. – I can dig that – there's something about Stravinsky you don't like – yeah?"

"O.K. All together now ..."

HEY MAESTRO! SHOW US YER FIDDLE!

"Why is he biting your leg? He is biting your leg because you are murdering Beethoven."

"No wonder you didn't go down very well – that's the manager's electric razor!"

"He's so dumb – he thinks fortissimo is something only played in castles."

"The overbearing tonality of the glissando indicated too greater reliance on technical trickery? You hated it - right?"

"Well – the cat doesn't like it, that's for sure."

"If it's such an old radio, how come it's playing modern music?"

"Don't call us ... we'll call you ..."

"And now – recalling last winter's successful tour of the supermarket car park, Bruch's Violin Concerto No. 1."

"*What kind of platform management leaves the lid down?*"

"Say aah …"

"The piano teacher gave us our money back plus another fifty not to take him any more!"

"*So, he's a little odd. A good harpist is hard to find ...*"

"What is happening to tenors? Even on a box you're too little!"

"*So you can write music …*"

"... can't everybody?"

"O.K. – it's a difficult orchestra, but do I really need a bodyguard?"

"That's the last time we use real cannon in the 1812."

"Frankly, solo bass drum is not something I get asked for ..."

"He thinks a steel band is one that uses stolen equipment ..."

"He gets very bored during other people's solos."

"course I can read music – M-U-S-I-C. It's some of them longer words that throw me …"

"Joshua – it's a bill from Jericho City Council!"

"So I stopped before anyone else – does that matter? After all, it is the Unfinished Symphony."

"Apparently this new conductor is very laid back ..."

"*Another advantage of having immense wealth son is being able to play the slide trombone stark naked from your own balcony!*"

"Play it again, Sam!"

"Why are you playing 'Romeo and Juliet' – why not join the rest of us in the 'Pathetique'?"

*"Ladies and Gentlemen, we should like to play Beethoven's 5th Symphony
.. We'd like to, but we can't, so we're doing 'Chopsticks' instead."*

"How about that – 'Air on a Drawstring'!"

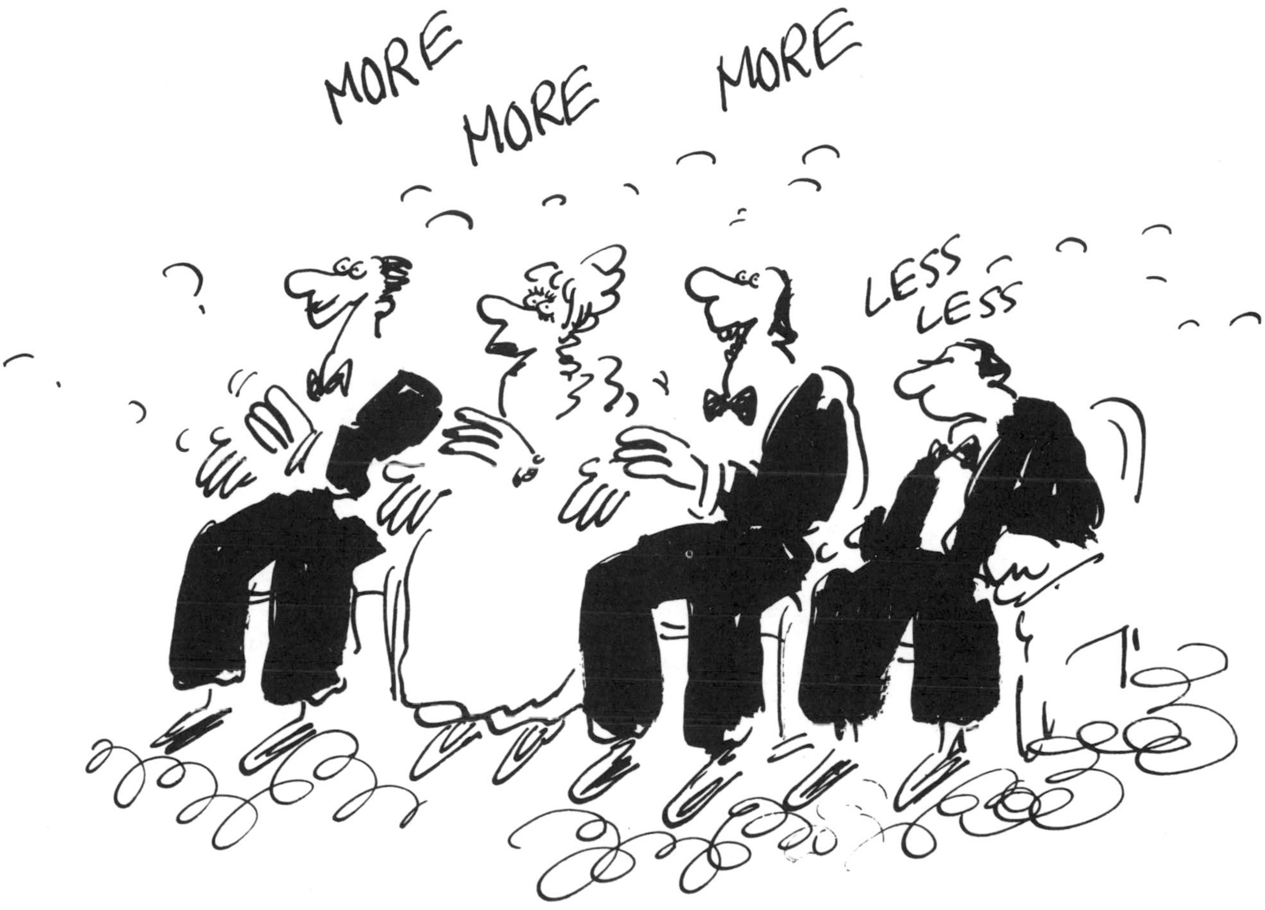
MORE
MORE
MORE
LESS
LESS

"If you let her play on <u>your</u> dentures, she's going to think she can do it on everybody's."

"*Mr.Finingham jumped up and down on my clarinet, gave me all his money and made me promise not to come again.*"

"*I am the ghost of Frederic Chopin and I'll thank you to stop ruining my nocturne!*"

"I know! Let's have a sing-song around the piano!"

"Go on Trevor – 'The Bells of St. Mary' one more time for Mrs.Strimmington ..."

"Let's face it dear, we've got a tone deaf dog!"

"Tchaikovsky? He can't even <u>spell</u> it!"

"A bum note? We don't have bum notes up here ..."

"You can't call it 'The sitting on a little hillock symphony' Ludwig – how about 'Pastorale'?"

"And now – for all the experts who applauded that last piece, I'll play it again with the music the right way up …"

"The way they treat their pets is terrible, listen to it screaming."

"*What on earth are you doing in there – it sounds like you've got the cat by the tail …*"

"*I said – stop crunching those mints!*"

"*Course when you hear the same piece on CD you're immediately struck by the richer, more dynamic sound and the subtleties which one just doesn't hear on a normal system ...*"

"Here is the score. Please try to blow your nose <u>only</u> where it says 'Brass'."

"It's just your father's way of saying he'd like you to take up chess."

"Just because I mentioned that I thought the saxophone had a sexy sound doesn't mean that ..."

"*Well, he did get it wrong three times in a row ...*"

"It does tape, records, radio, compact disc and toasted sandwiches."

"*Looks like we got another job creation percussionist ..*"

"Most people snore or talk in their sleep – you can play piano concertos ..."

"I said – nobody lives next door!"

"*Will you stop coughing!!*"

"Violin by Stradivarius – hands by Von Frankenstein!"

"*I have lost the music for tonight's avant garde piece. Instead I shall drain this bottle of vodka, blindfold myself and play the piano with my feet. The effect is much the same.*"

"Hey man – how about pounding the ceiling in time with the music?"

Other books in the "Crazy World" series:

The Crazy World of Birdwatching. £3.99. By Peter Rigby. Over eighty cartoons on the strange antics of the twitcher brigade. One of our most popular pastimes, this will be a natural gift for any birdwatcher.

The Crazy World of Gardening. £3.99. By Bill Stott. The perfect present for anyone who has ever wrestled with a lawnmower that won't start, over-watered a pot plant or been assaulted by a rose bush from behind.

The Crazy World of Golf. £3.99. By Mike Scott. Over eighty hilarious cartoons show the fanatic golfer in his (or her) every absurdity. What really goes on out on the course, and the golfer's life when not playing are chronicled in loving detail.

The Crazy World of The Handyman. £3.99. By Roland Fiddy. This book is a must for anyone who has ever hung *one* length of wallpaper upside down or drilled through an electric cable. A gift for anyone who has ever tried to "do it yourself" and failed!

The Crazy World of Jogging. £3.99. By David Pye. An ideal present for all those who find themselves running early in the morning in the rain and wondering why they're there. They will find their reasons, their foibles and a lot of laughs in this collection.

The Crazy World of Love. £3.99. By Roland Fiddy. This funny yet tender collection covers every aspect of love from its first joys to its dying embers. An ideal gift for lovers of all ages to share with each other.

The Crazy World of Marriage. £3.99. By Bill Stott. The battle of the sexes in close-up from the altar to the grave, in public and in private, in and out of bed. See your friends, your enemies (and possibly yourselves?) as never before!

The Crazy World of Photography. £3.99. By Bill Stott. Everyone who owns a camera, be it a Box Brownie or the latest Pentax, will find something to laugh at in this superb collection. The absurdities of the camera freak will delight your whole family.

The Crazy World of Rugby. £3.99. By Bill Stott. From schoolboy to top international player, no-one who plays or watches rugby (or who washes the kit afterwards) will not enjoy this book. Over 80 hilarious cartoons – a must for all addicts.

The Crazy World of Sailing. £3.99. By Peter Rigby. The perfect present for anyone who has ever messed about in boats, gone pea-green in a storm or been stuck in the doldrums.

The Crazy World of Sex. £3.99. By David Pye. A light-hearted look at the absurdities and weaker moments of human passion – the turn-ons and the turn-offs. Very funny and in (reasonably) good taste.

The Crazy World of Skiing. £3.99. By Craig Peterson and Jerry Emerson. Covering almost every possible (and impossible) experience on the slopes, this is an ideal present for anyone who has ever strapped on skis – and instantly fallen over. "A riotous suggestion … very funny and very original." (The Good Book Guide)

The Crazy World of Tennis. £3.99. By Peter Rigby. Would-be Pat Cashes and Chris Everts watch out…. This brilliant collection will pinpoint their pretensions and poses. Whether you play yourself or only watch on TV, this will amuse and entertain you!

United Kingdom

These books make super presents. Order them from your local bookseller or from Exley Publications Ltd, Dept BP, 16 Chalk Hill, Watford, Herts WD1 4BN. (Please send £1.00 to cover post and packing.)

United States

All these titles are distributed in the United States by Slawson Communications Inc., 165 Vallecitos de Oro, San Marcos, CA 92069 and are priced at $8.95 each.